Birds /   142103
E598 O'Ha

O'Hare, Ted,
Wilton Public Library

Birds

WHAT IS AN ANIMAL?

Ted O'Hare

Rourke

Publishing LLC

Vero Beach, Florida 32964

www.rourkepublishing.com

PHOTO CREDITS: All photos © Lynn M. Stone

Title page: A Florida scrub jay perches in a scrub oak forest.

Editor: Frank Sloan

Cover and interior design by Nicola Stratford

Library of Congress Cataloging-in-Publication Data

O'Hare, Ted, 1961-
    Birds / Ted O'Hare.
        p. cm. -- (What is an animal?)
    Includes bibliographical references and index.
    ISBN 1-59515-416-7 (hardcover)
    1. Birds--Juvenile literature. I. Title. II. Series: O'Hare, Ted,
1961-   What is an animal?
    QL676.2.O36 2006
    598--dc22

Printed in the USA

CG/CG

Rourke Publishing

www.rourkepublishing.com – sales@rourkepublishing.com
Post Office Box 3328, Vero Beach, FL 32964
1-800-394-7055

Table of Contents

Birds

Birds are **vertebrates** because they have backbones. Birds are animals with feathers and wings. Most birds use their wings to fly. Some birds, however, cannot fly.

Birds do not have teeth. They are **warm-blooded**. This means they keep a steady body temperature in any kind of weather.

Wings and air-filled, hollow bones allow this roseate spoonbill to fly.

Bird Habits

Most birds travel long distances. They may live in the north and then fly south for the winter. These journeys are known as **migrations**.

Many birds migrate, but the Arctic tern goes the longest distance. It flies 11,000 miles (17,700 kilometers) from the Arctic to the Antarctic and back each year.

Snow geese migrate each fall from Canada to the south.

Kinds of Birds

Scientists have found nearly 10,000 bird **species**. Nearly 700 of them live in North America. They may be as small as the tiny hummingbird. Or they may be as large as swans that weigh 30 pounds (13.5 kilograms).

Scientists say there are 21 major groups of birds. They group birds largely by body shapes, features, and habits.

DiD YoU KNoW?

The best-known bird group includes the family of hawks, eagles, and vultures.

The king vulture of Latin America is one kind of bird of prey.

9

Where Birds Live

Birds live in almost every known **habitat**. Habitats are living places such as marshes, ponds, and prairies. Most species live in warm, tropical habitats.

Several kinds of penguins and petrels live on or near Antarctica. Penguins have dense feathers and a layer of fat. These keep them warm.

King penguins live in groups on islands near Antarctica.

Baby swans follow their parents, but they feed themselves.

The black skimmer nests on the ground. Its eggs are the color of sandy soil.

Bird Bodies

Each bird species has a body that works well for its habitat. A bird's build tells much about where it lives and what it eats.

A bird with long legs is most likely a wader. A bird that dives is shaped like a torpedo. A bird with webbed feet lives in a watery habitat.

DiD YOU KNOW?

A bird with **talons** and a sharp beak is a hunter.

A pelican's bill is designed to make catching fish easy.

Amazing Birds

Cranes dance. Emperor penguins lay their eggs in the Antarctic cold. Some vultures break open bones by dropping them while they fly.

The ostrich weighs 300 pounds (140 kilograms). Its floppy wings are useless for flight, but it runs like a deer. The male prairie chicken has a pouch on its throat to call mates.

The keel-billed toucan has a bill that looks like a banana.

Predator and Prey

Some birds are true **predators**. They kill other animals, their **prey**, so they have food. Eagles attack fish and small land animals.

Some birds become prey. Many young birds are taken from nests by bobcats, raccoons, snakes, and other hunters.

DiD YOU KNOW?

Some **falcons** attack other birds, striking them with their talons.

A bald eagle grabs a fish with its talons.

Baby Birds

Mother birds lay eggs, usually in a nest. The adult's feathers keep the eggs warm. Then they hatch.

Most birds stay in the nest for several days or weeks. The parents bring food to them. Most young birds can fly in just a few weeks.

DID YOU KNOW?
Geese and cranes leave their nests shortly after they hatch.

A wood stork feeds its chicks partly digested food.

21

People and Birds

Birds are important to people in North America. People use birds for food, for sport, and as pets. By studying birds' flight, early people learned how to build flying machines.

Many birds are in danger of disappearing. Birds can be protected if we take care of their habitats.

GLOSSARY

falcons (FAL kunz) — slender hawks with narrow wings for quick flight

habitat (HAB uh TAT) — a special kind of place where an animal lives

migrations (my GRAY shunz) — long journeys certain animals may take, usually at the same time each year

predators (PRED uh terz) — animals that hunt other animals for food

prey (PRAY) — an animal that is hunted by other animals for food

species (SPEE sheez) — within a group of closely related animals, one certain kind, such as a trumpeter swan

talons (TAL unz) — the toe claws of birds of prey such as eagles

vertebrates (VER tuh BRAYTZ) — animals with backbones; fish, amphibians, reptiles, birds, and mammals are vertebrates

warm-blooded (WARM BLUD ed) — refers to birds and mammals, animals whose bodies keep a steady, warm temperature even in cold weather

Index

Further Reading

Arlon, Penelope. *DK First Animal Encyclopedia*. Dorling Kindersley, 2004
Pascoe, Elaine. *Animals with Backbones*. Powerkids Press, 2003
Solway, Andrew. *Classifying Birds*. Heinemann Library, 2003

Websites to Visit

http://www.biologybrowser.org
http://www.kidport.com/RefLib/Science/Animals/AnimalIndexV.htm
http://nationalzoo.si.edu/Animals/Birds/ForKids

About the Author

Ted O'Hare is an author and editor of children's books. He divides his time between New York City and a home upstate.